TRAGEDY OF SUICIDE

THE PURPOSE OF EARTH LIFE

PAUL E. CHU

ISBN 0-931610-05-2
Library of Congress Catalog
  Card Number 92-90907

Printed in the United States
of America
World View Press
P.O.Box 1314
Englewood Cliffs, NJ 07632

THE TRAGEDY OF SUICIDE

THE PURPOSE OF EARTH LIFE

PAUL E. CHU

Copyright © 1992 by Paul E. Chu
Printed in the United States of America
World View Press, Box 1314,
Englewood Cliffs, N.J. 07632
All Rights Reserved

TRAGEDY OF SUICIDE

Table of Contents

The Tragedy of Suicide	1
The Difference Between the Living and the Dead	2
The Etheric Body or the Body of Living Formative Forces	4
The Etheric Body of the Plant	7
Man Awake versus Man in Deep Sleep	8
The Astral Body	10
The EGO	12
Man's Unconscionable Acts	13
Man's "DOUBLE"	17
What Happens to Man's Four Members After Death	21
The Physical Body After Death Is Left by Itself	22
The Physical Body After Death	22
The Etheric Body After Death	23

The Astral Body and Ego After Death	24
The Tragic Act of the Suicide	26
The Situation of the Suicide's Soul After Death	28
Isolation of the Astral Body And Ego of the Suicide	30
Period of Loneliness	31
Lovers Suicide to be Together Defeated	31
A Little Help for the Suicide's Soul	32
Consequences for the Suicide's Future	32
The Further Progress of the Astral Body and Ego in the Astral World After Death	34

The Moon Sphere, Venus Sphere and Mercury Sphere	34
The Venus Sphere	36
The Ego's Progress Into the "World of Spirit" The Sun Sphere	44
The Second Region of Spiritland	47
Other Regions of Spiritland	47
The Cosmic Guide Into the Land of Spirits, The Zodiac	49
What the Spiritual Beings Create for Man and Woman	51
The Cosmic Midnight	52
The Ego's Return From the Zodiac Toward Earth	54
The Spiritual Orb of the Seed of the Physical Body	55
The Ego's Return From the Zodiac to the Solar System	57

The Sphere of the Outer Planets	59
The Sun Sphere and the Inner Planets	59
Return to the Moon Sphere	60
The New Earth Life	62
The Cosmic Source of the Child	63
The Reincarnating Human Being	64
The Tempters of Man: Lucifer and Ahriman	66
Lucifer's Aims	67
Ahriman's Aims	68
The Etheric Christ	69
The Power of Ahriman	71
Current Ideas of Modern Man	74
What is Needed of Mankind	75
More of Ahriman's Plans	78
Luciferic Beings	80
Man The Battleground	80
Ahriman's Forthcoming Incarnation	81

Reincarnation and Karma	83
The Purpose of Earthlife	85
The Consciousness Soul Age	86
Reincarnation as a Logical Process	87
MY ORIGIN AND YOURS	91

THE TRAGEDY OF SUICIDE

The tragedy of suicide is that a living human being is suddenly destroyed. One's own life willfully ended. In what way? In a way that leaves all the desires, hopes, problems, and wishes still unfulfilled, and ignores all the years and years of care that most mothers and fathers gave to raise a child just to adolescence. Consider the nine months that the embryo must develop in the mother's body. She undergoes discomfort of many kinds and must make sacrifices every moment during that period. Everyone has seen graphically on TV scenes the pain the mother undergoes at the birth of the child. Nurses and doctors are also needed at birth.

After birth there are many 24-hour days when both parents must care for a sick child. Even a child who is not sick requires constant care and attention. Raising and caring for a child from birth to the crawling stage, then to the crawling-standing-walking stage, through learning to talk, finding the meaning of every word in his vocabulary.... all these have taken the direct efforts of dozens and hundreds of people. Taken together with the food we eat, books we read, cars we ride, roads we use, it includes the whole world in which we live!

THE DIFFERENCE BETWEEN THE LIVING AND THE DEAD

The suicide destroys his physical body. When the physical body dies, it does not mean that nothing of the person exists anymore. In order to understand this, let us take the case of a person who dies in his sleep.

At the moment that a person dies in his sleep, all the parts of the physical body are still there. Physically, we see that he has stopped breathing, and on taking his pulse, we know that his heart has stopped beating. And the doctor would pronounce him "dead".

As soon as death takes place, the physical body begins to decompose into the inorganic elements of the earth.If the body is buried, the process takes a period of time. If cremated,the body returns to its elements quickly.

On the other hand, a person who is asleep shows there are LIFE FORCES within him. His heart is beating, blood is coursing through his veins which we can see if we watch carefully. We can also see the rise and fall of his chest as the life forces of his lungs continually keep him united with the world of air surrounding him.

THE ETHERIC BODY
OR THE
BODY OF LIVING FORMATIVE FORCES

The forces that keep the heart beating and the lungs breathing and which are in every single organ of the body, form a single unified member in every man and woman. This is an invisible member of man's being. It is called the ETHERIC BODY, or body of formative life forces. Without these life forces, you have only a corpse. During sleep, the etheric body remains in the physical body. It sustains life, rebuilds the worn-out body and even heals the ills of the body.

The etheric body enters the embryo soon after conception and remains united with the physical body throughout life until death. At death, the etheric body LEAVES the physical body. The latter then dies and becomes a corpse.

When you cut your finger, the etheric body immediately sets to work and in a few days, the finger looks as good as new, or as if nothing had happened to it. Consciously, you had nothing to do with the healing, except probably to clean it and bandage it.

If you break a leg skiing, the doctor set the bones, makes a cast and "let's nature take its course". This "nature" that the doctor sets his trust and his faith in to do the actual rebuilding of the broken bone, join the blood vessels, muscles, tendons, skin and numerous other cells, is none other than the unique etheric body of man.

In the babe, the etheric body builds the physical body so that it grows visibly in size as the days go by. The COSMIC WISDOM embodied in the etheric body sets the time for each stage of growth, as when the baby teeth form, grow, decay to make room for the permanent adult teeth; the start of puberty and every stage of human development.

THE ETHERIC BODY OF THE PLANT

The plant also has an etheric body and is a living plant. When the etheric body separates, the plant dies and becomes wood. The etheric body of the giant redwoods which grow hundreds of feet high, is the force that draws the redwood sap hundreds of feet above the ground.

The maximum height that atmospheric pressure can force water to rise in a vacuum is about 34 feet, equivalent to the height of 29.92 inches of mercury that the weather forecaster reports as barometric pressure.

So you can see that the etheric body of a living tree as the redwood or any tall tree is much more powerful than that of atmospheric pressure to cause the sap to rise to the top of the tree. Many sequoia exceed 300 feet in height. If it had to depend on atmospheric pressure for its sap to rise to its higher branches, it would never grow to such startling heights.

We will return later to follow the course of the etheric body of man after death. It is necessary to consider another unseen member of man's being at this point.

MAN AWAKE versus MAN IN DEEP SLEEP

In order to understand another of man's unseen members, we must consider the difference between man who is awake and the same man in deep sleep.

A person who is awake is conscious of things around him. He sees objects, hears sounds, music or whatever is taking place. He may be watching TV, or talking to people. In all these, he is conscious. He shows sympathy or antipathy. He has feelings of love for some, hate for others. He has desires for food or drink, alcohol or even drugs.

In deep sleep, all these disappear. He is unconscious until he awakes. There could even be a party going on around him and he would know nothing about it.

Why is that so? The body is still there. The heart is still beating, breathing is still going on. All that our physical senses know of the waking man are still present in the sleeping man. You can weigh the awake man and the sleeping man and they will weigh exactly the same.

So why is it that the wide-awake-man has consciousness of his surroundings whereas the sleeping man who appears to have all the same physical organs and weighs exactly the same, does NOT have any consciousness of his surroundings?

THE ASTRAL BODY

The answer must be that man has an INVISIBLE, WEIGHTLESS member which is the BEARER of his consciousness, feelings, desires, etc. and that this invisible member must have LEFT THE PHYSICAL BODY DURING SLEEP.

As a matter of fact, human beings who have developed their

higher faculties, can see this ordinarily invisible member of man. This member is called the ASTRAL BODY. It is related to the astral world or starry and planetary world to which it must return daily in order to replenish its forces. If you do not believe the last statement, try staying awake for three or four days.

At death, this astral body, together with other invisible members of man, separate from the physical body and continue their life in higher worlds.

This will be explained later, as we must consider here man's most important member, his ETERNAL SPIRIT, HIS EGO.

THE EGO

When a human being says "I", he or she points to a unique being: HIMSELF! or HERSELF! Each one can say "I" and mean only himself or herself. The word cannot refer to any being except the one who says it.

This "I" is the EGO, the eternal SPIRIT of each one of us. This ego is a part of the COSMIC EGO which was "breathed" into man by God after man had developed into a condition when he could develop individually and consciously. This ego is a part of the COSMIC EGO which was given to each and every human being for him and for her to develop on earth through numerous lives in order to raise it to a divine, let's be brash and say, "angelic" state.

Now that we've said it, how many say: "It can't be so!" Shall we point to some out of the masses of humanity who are headed that way? For a starter, how about Florence Nightingale, St. Francis of Assisi, Mother Teresa?

You will note there is NO football player, no basketball player, no baseball player, no boxer, actress, actor, newscaster, CEO, judge, head of state or singer on the list (although I do not know whether Florence sings like a nightingale).

MAN'S UNCONSCIONABLE ACTS

In contrast to the few examples mentioned above, it is possible for anyone to list thousands and thousands of humanity who are headed in the opposite direction: straight to hell.

In every newspaper every day, week after week, month after month, year after year we read or hear about horrible murders, rapes, knifing, brutal prison conditions in countries all over the world, shelling of defenseless people, bombing of crowded areas, bankers robbing elderly of their life savings, and lawyers doing the same.

More examples must be mentioned because people take their actions so lightly, whereas, the most serious consequences result from our acts.

If a person offers a youngster cocaine or some other drug, and if the one who accepts it develops a habit and falls deeper and deeper into its use and finally succumbs to its effects, the one who initiated the use of the drug has ruined a life. He cannot escape the consequences of his irresponsible act.

Or take the businessmen who advertise their cigarettes as virile, macho-symbols and snare young boys and girls to take up smoking and develop a habit that leads to emphysema and lung cancer. There are hordes of humanity dying daily from the effects of cigarette smoking and still millions of dollars are spent on ads extolling the use of cigarettes. That is done not only in this country, but the advertising is carried on in poor developing countries also.

Apparently, these businessmen think it does NOT matter if the victims of their greed are some unknown, nameless, "foreign-looking" masses just as long as they can afford to buy their death-dealing product. However, how their "double" will appear to themselves and others will not be a pretty picture.

Even countries like Taipei are appealing to citizens of this country to urge our so-called enlightened government to prevent our greedy cigarette manufacturers from flooding Taipei with enticing ads for cigarettes!

Manufacturers of guns and those working to maximize their ownership, know how deadly their products are, and they too will see how many deaths they cause.

The list can go on and on, but I believe the above gives you an idea of the staggering extent of the evil that man does to man. Why is this so?

One of the main reasons is that humanity has lost sight of his SPIRITUAL origin and now considers that birth is the beginning of life, and death is the end of existence. He does not even know that he has an ego, an astral body, and an etheric body, but thinks he is only a physical body evolved from the apes.

MAN'S "DOUBLE"

Here is a shocker you will not find in your textbooks in high school, college, or graduate school.

DURING MAN'S ENTIRE LIFE ON EARTH, he continually creates an invisible, supersensible being which shows in its physiognomy, in its facial and bodily features, his moral qualities. If he thinks evil thoughts, has evil feelings, does evil deeds, these immediately show in the evil, horrible appearance of that "double". This "double" can be seen by one who has developed the necessary faculties. The "double" of evil-doers take fantastically fearful shapes more frightful than any imagined in the physical world. If a person is unprepared and sees this being, he could be overwhelmed by the sight, and may not even associate it with himself.

The novel ZANONI by Bulwer-Lytton is a depiction of a "double". This is one description from that novel: "It gazes on thee, the dark, mantled, loathsome thing! There, there, there with their devilish mockery and hateful craft, glare on thee those horrid eyes."

After death, man sees his "double" and he also learns that he himself created it and that his task is to transform that evil-looking being into one of beauty by his own deeds. This being is the bearer of our Karma, our destiny. Just think how surprised those evil doers in life on earth will be when they die and find that all their evil deeds are registered in their features and their form!

People commit murder every day and night. Most of them probably hope they will never be caught. Many do escape the law while on earth, BUT they can NEVER, NEVER escape the horrible "double" that accompanies them after death!

In the astral world that first extends to the Moon sphere, that is, to the space from the earth to the orbit of the moon around the earth, sympathy and antipathy rule. That is, the soul with an evil physiognomy can only approach those of like physiognomy. Whereas on earth, we humans can normally approach the good as well as the evil, because the evil can hide behind a mask of semi-solid flesh, that is not the case in the astral world.

After death the "double's" hideous form cannot be hidden. It is there for all to see. There will be NO clever lawyer there to plead its innocence. There will be NO plastic surgeon to alter the face and form of the "double". There will be no stupid man-made laws to fall back on to claim "innocent because of insanity". If one allies oneself with the devil, it is one's own free choice, and it shows in his physiognomy.

Consider the terrorists who bomb planes and buildings with great loss of life. The terrorists' earth-bound thinking supposes that they have performed great heroic deeds and their compatriots reward them lavishly. BUT their astral bodies and egos have become evil and their "double" will haunt them unmercifully until they themselves change it.

WHAT HAPPENS TO MAN'S FOUR MEMBERS AFTER DEATH

Now that we have mentioned the four members of man (there are three higher members which we need not consider here): the ego, astral body, etheric body and physical body, we can discuss briefly what happens to each of these members after death.

THE PHYSICAL BODY AFTER DEATH
IS LEFT BY ITSELF

After death, the etheric body, astral body, ego and "double" LEAVE the physical body. The person is then lifeless. The separation of the three higher members can be caused by illness, old age, or any of the numerous means available to the suicide.

THE PHYSICAL BODY AFTER DEATH

The physical body then returns to the mineral state at various rates, depending on innumerable factors. The rate can be slowed considerably by cryogenics, the use of liquid nitrogen to freeze the body.

THE ETHERIC BODY AFTER DEATH

The etheric body, besides being the body of life forces, also is the carrier of man's memory. At death, the etheric body gives the astral body and ego with which it is still united, a panoramic review of the life just ended. Starting from the moment of death, the review goes backward to birth. This review takes about three days. The etheric body can then no longer keep from expanding outward into the etheric cosmos with which it then unites. An essence of the etheric body becomes a part of the ego.

How can cryogenic-man recapture the etheric body which has expanded into the universe? The possibility is the same as that of a cowboy lassoing the moon.

THE ASTRAL BODY AND EGO AFTER DEATH

After the panoramic review of the life just ended, the astral body and ego live together and are connected for a long period: many, many years, in the normal death event. The soul still has many desires, wishes and hopes unfulfilled which are connected with the physical body. For example, hunger and thirst, desire for food and drink: for a beer, a coke, or a steak....you name yours, are needs of a physical body, but the desires are in the soul. They are in the astral body, and the astral body lives on in the astral world after the physical body is dead.

In life, by having the food and drink in the physical body, those desires of the astral body are satisfied.

After death, there is NO physical body to take in the food and drink, so the soul goes literally through hell with those unfulfilled desires.

How does it feel to have a longing for anything, unfulfilled? We see smokers on buses on long trips who cannot wait to get off at any stop so that they can get a puff. We hear of those on drugs who agonize because they cannot get a shot. The reader, no doubt, can give innumerable examples of those who literally "go through hell" because some desire cannot be fulfilled.

So it is with the astral body with its many earthly desires which can no longer be satisfied because after death, the astral body and ego no longer have a physical body as their companion.

THE TRAGIC ACT OF THE SUICIDE

Now that we have some idea of man as a physical being and of his higher members, that is, his etheric body, astral body and ego, we can begin to discuss why it is a great tragedy for a human being to commit suicide.

Firstly, all the problems leading to the suicide are still there. Killing the body does NOT destroy the desires and wishes leading to the suicide. If the cause is hopelessness in the situation in life, it will be shown later, in considering the further progress of the astral body and ego after death, that this particular physical body, and the environment in which the ego lives, were specifically chosen by the ego for its development at this stage of his evolving. By overcoming the problems encountered in those conditions of life in which he finds himself, he develops the faculties and talents which he needs to bring about progress for himself in the future.

Even if poverty and illness are his lot, the overcoming of poverty and illness strengthens him and gives him added forces and talents for his future development, even if the problems result in death in this life.

You may gather from that statement that there are future lives. That is definitely so and will be discussed more fully later. It is also necessary to know that egos have also had lives in the past. What they did then are the causes of their present life conditions.

THE SITUATION OF THE SUICIDE'S SOUL AFTER DEATH

What happens to the astral body and ego of the suicide after death? Cutting off life, SEVERING THE PHYSICAL BODY by a sudden act of suicide, especially by the young, leaves countless very strong desires, countless wishes, etc. unfulfilled, and unfulfillable. That is, IMPOSSIBLE TO BE FULFILLED because there is NO physical body to eat the food, drink the coke, even if the food and drink are physically available.

What a horrible, horrible situation to be in! All the wishes, desires and unfulfilled wants leading to the suicide are still there, but there is no physical body anymore. The body could be shattered, poisoned, or in whatever condition the suicide decided, or even not found. For the soul and ego of the suicide, the result is the same: NO PHYSICAL BODY. No body to feed, to cure the "hopeless" situation with, whatever the situation may be.

Could it be hunger? Unrequited love? (Or is it self-love?) Inability to acquire the job? The car? The home? The mate? The attention? The status?

Whatever the reason may be, the body is gone, but the underlying causes are still within the soul. Therefore, they outlast the death of the physical body.

And the astral body and ego of the suicide? They DO NOT

immediately follow the course of the person who dies a natural death.

ISOLATION OF THE ASTRAL BODY AND EGO OF THE SUICIDE

Rudolf Steiner, the SEER and initiate, on following the course of the soul of the suicide says "the suicide, by taking that desperate step, actually casts his soul and ego into a most devastating situation of entering the soul world before its allotted time (the individual's normal life span). Therefore, the suicide's soul and ego are as (if) in a prison sealed off from other soul/egos who are rightfully in that world at that time.

The state of being cut off from other soul/egos is described as "being of utmost loneliness, cut off from any communication with all beings. It is a situation, which if known beforehand, would cause the suicide NOT TO RESORT TO SUCH AN ACT".

PERIOD OF LONELINESS

The period of such loneliness lasts as long as the normal life span would have lasted.

LOVERS' SUICIDE TO BE TOGETHER DEFEATED

Two lovers may think that they will be united immediately after committing suicide. Could it be that each is separated completely from each other and from every other soul? If, because of the self-destructive act, each soul is in isolation until his or her natural death should take place, then the very purpose of the suicide in order to be together after death would be defeated.

A LITTLE HELP FOR THE SUICIDE'S SOUL

If a person is cognizant of the fate of the suicide's soul as stated above, he can send his strong love forces to that soul by concentrating and thinking of him or her with his heart forces.

CONSEQUENCES FOR THE SUICIDE'S FUTURE

The act of suicide is a momentous, shattering, decisive act. It is based on one's very limited earthly knowledge of what the purpose of his or her present earthlife is. The decision is based on narrow, dimmed-down, finite, earth-bound points of view.

In contrast, cosmic beings of sublime wisdom had prepared, on the basis of what the ego had brought to them from the ego's previous earth-life, the spiritual forces which formed the spiritual seed of his physical body and the destiny needed by him for this life on earth.

This will be explained further under the subject of the life of the ego in the spirit world.

By the act of the suicide, all the wisdom of sublime spiritual beings are shattered and brought to naught. Suicide, is therefore, also a cosmic tragedy.

THE FURTHER PROGRESS OF THE ASTRAL BODY AND EGO IN THE ASTRAL WORLD AFTER DEATH

In earth life, the soul is intimately connected with the physical body. It therefore takes into itself the joys and pleasures of the physical body in all its forms. After death, it lives in the soul world with the ego, whose true world is the spirit world. In order for the ego to proceed to the spirit world, the soul must get rid of all the ties it has to the physical world and to the physical body.

THE MOON SPHERE, VENUS SPHERE AND MERCURY SPHERE

There are seven regions in the soul world where the various

connections the soul has to earth-life are severed. To one who has clung little to the physical life, the period will be short. To one for whom earth life is everything and the only thing, the period will be long.

The lowest region entered by the soul is where the coarsest, lowest selfish desires of the physical life are felt most strongly, and are purged. This is the region of Burning Desires. The term correctly and accurately describes the condition of the soul in that region.

The soul eventually learns to overcome those desires and not to yearn for what can only be satisfied with a physical body. The Seer says that "it is a dark and gloomy state in which the soul finds itself". Those with few lusts go through it without noticing it, for they have no affinity with it.

In the second region, losing oneself in the external glitter of life, the joy in the swiftly succeeding impressions of the senses, the worthless trifles of life must be extinguished. Without the body and the physical objects needed for the satisfaction of these desires, the state of suffering can be intense. The state of suffering itself leads to the conquest of these earthly ties.

THE VENUS SPHERE

The astral body and ego progress to the VENUS sphere which extends outward from earth to the orbit of Venus as a radius. In the Venus sphere work the spirits of illness and death which bring illness and death not in old age, but in the flower of youth or in childhood through epidemics and illnesses of manifold types.

There the Seer sees with painful sorrow how those souls who on earth spent a life without a conscience, each condemn himself to become a servant of these evil beings of illness and death who send these destructive forces into our world.

The traits of laziness also have their after effects in the Venus sphere. Human beings having this laziness trait sentence themselves to bear the yoke of slavery to the spirits of hindrance who work on the earth. These evil spirits are under the domination of AHRIMAN. (See following section on Ahriman and Lucifer).

Those of moral character on earth easily make contact with those with whom they were united on earth. Those lacking moral qualities on earth find difficulty making such contact.

In the astral world, up through the Mercury sphere, the astral body and ego re-experience the past life intensely, from the point of death backward to birth. The ego is intensely conscious of the effects of his earthly deeds upon those who had suffered from his deeds. In the body-free existence, the personal earthly reactions are no longer as they were on earth, but are experienced from the point of view of the ones who were harmed. Therefore, the harm he had done appear in their true dimension, and he makes strong intentions to correct all his misdeeds.

He knows those evil deeds had caused his "double's" evil appearance and he looks forward for the opportunity to correct all his misdeeds. This, you will find can only be done on earth in a new physical body.

Just think that if men on earth were aware of their "double's" evil appearance where everyone can see them, would there be all the crimes we see today and will continue to see as time goes on?

In the third region, the wish nature predominates. At death, there may be many wishes unfulfilled. In this region, those wishes must die out because of the impossibility of their being fulfilled.

The fourth region of the soul is one of Attraction and Repulsion. When the soul is in the physical body, it feels attracted to those things and conditions which serve its liking and well-being. It is repulsed by those which displeases it. These are based mainly on the bodily nature of man. After death, there is NO body to give this feeling of self, so the soul feels emptied out. A feeling as if it had lost itself overcomes the soul. This continues until it recognizes that the true man does not lie in the physical. It must come to the fact that the corporeal is not the essential reality.

It should not pass unnoticed that the experiences of this region are suffered to an especial degree by suicides. They leave their physical body in an artificial way, while nevertheless all the feelings connected with it remain unchanged. In the case of natural death, the decay of the body is accompanied by a partial dying out of the feelings of attachment to it. In the case of suicides, there are, in addition to the torment caused by the feeling of having been suddenly emptied out, the unsatisfied desires and wishes on account of which they have deprived themselves of their bodies.

In the fifth stage, enthusiasm for nature in a sensuous way undergoes cleansing. This sensuous love of nature must be distinguished from the love of nature which seeks for the spirit which reveals itself in the things and events of nature. Even religious observances sought only for their sensuous welfare must be purified in this region.

In the sixth region, the part of the soul which thirsts for action because the action affords them sensuous satisfaction must be purified. Even idealists who crave action because of the sensuous satisfaction they derive from the action, are in this category, as well as those of artistic natures who delve into scientific activity because it pleases them.

The seventh region frees man from the last inclinations to the physical sense world. Here is the belief that man's activity should be devoted entirely to the physical world. The idea that nothing exists beyond the material world and that all one does must be connected only with the physical world, must be destroyed in this region. There the "souls see that no objects exist in true reality for materialistic thinking. Like ice in the sun this belief of the soul melts away. The soul being is now absorbed into its own world; the spirit free from all its fetters rises to the region where it lives in its own surroundings only. The soul has completed its previous earthly task, and after death any traces of this task that remained fettering the spirit, have dissolved. By overcoming the last trace of the earth, the soul is itself given back to its own element".

When the re-experiencing of the last life from death backwards to birth has been completed, it will have taken from twenty to thirty years, or one third of the length of the life just ended. The period of one dying in childhood would be much shorter, while that of a babe would be negligible.

The astral body and ego in the meantime would have expanded through the Moon sphere, Venus sphere and Mercury sphere.

THE EGO'S PROGRESS INTO THE "WORLD OF SPIRIT" THE SUN SPHERE

The "World of the Spirit" is so unlike anything in the physical world that whatever we hear about it from one who has developed the senses to investigate it consciously, will appear fantastic. " Since our language is able to describe physical realities mainly, what is related of the spirit world is in analogies."

At the very beginning, one reads about the spirit world that "this world is woven out of the substance of which human thought consists. But thought, as it lives in man, is only a shadow picture, a phantom of its real being. As a shadow of an object on the wall is related to the real object that throws this shadow, so is the thought which makes its appearance through a human brain related to the being in the spiritland which corresponds to this thought. The awakened spiritual sense perceives this thought being just as the eye of the senses perceives the chair".

In the first region, are the spiritual Archetypes of all things and beings which are present in the physical and the soul worlds. What are these Archetypes? Imagine the picture of a painter existing in his mind before he paints it, even though he may not have all the details. This gives an idea of what is called an Archetype. In the spirit world, the

Archetypes are creative beings, constantly active, constantly creating.

All the physical things and beings are copies of these Archetypes. To the person with spiritual vision, these Archetypes are as real as your cat or dog is to you. Often innumerable Archetypes work together in order to bring about this or that being in the soul or physical world.

Accompanying all the creating, is an "ocean of tones", so seeing and sounding go together: the Pythagoreans' "MUSIC OF THE SPHERES".

THE SECOND REGION OF SPIRITLAND

The second region of spiritland contains the Archetypes of life. "It streams through the world of spirit like a fluid element, as it were like blood pulsating through all". It can be likened to the seas, but its distribution is more like the blood in the animal body. Here the Primal Forces produce everything that appear in physical reality as living beings: plants, animals, man.

OTHER REGIONS OF SPIRITLAND

In the third region the Archetypes of all soul formations are found. It is rarer than the first two regions, and may be called the air or atmosphere of spiritland. Here all feelings, sensations, instincts, passions, etc. are present, but in a spiritual way. The longing of the human soul appears as a gentle zephyr; loud storm and flashing lightning can be traced to the passions of a battle waged on earth.

The Archetypes of the fourth region govern the Archetypes of the three lower regions. They mediate their working together and a more comprehensive activity flow from them.

The Archetypes of the fifth, sixth and seventh regions supply the impulses for the activity of the lower regions. In them one finds the creative forces of the Archetypes themselves. He who can rise to these regions make contact with what can be called purposes which underlie our world. In these Archetypes, the most varied germinal thought beings are ready to be projected into the lower regions. The ideas which the human spirit work creatively are the reflection, the shadow of the germinal Thought-Beings of the higher worlds.

The ego's path leads through the spheres of MARS, JUPITER and SATURN. At the end of the Saturn sphere, the ego is at the portal into the vastness of the Zodiacal constellations.

THE COSMIC GUIDE INTO THE "LAND OF SPIRITS", THE ZODIAC

If on earth, man "had learned that the mighty Sun Spirit had entered into earth by descending into Jesus of Nazareth at the baptism in the Jordan and had lived through the

Mystery of Golgotha and had united Himself with earth since that time, then the Christ becomes the Guide of the ego into the bewildering complexities of the zodiacal constellations".

Here the ego lives as a spiritual being among the Mighty Hierarchies of the twelve constellations of the zodiac. Only the most advanced egos live among the Hierarchies consciously and take part in the stupendous task with the hierarchies in building the spiritual seed of the physical body required by the ego to fulfill its tasks in the forthcoming earth life. All the less developed egos must depend on the hierarchies to complete the tasks for them, according to what each ego brings to them from the last lives.

WHAT THE HIERARCHICAL BEINGS CREATE FOR MAN AND WOMAN

The forces from the Spiritual Beings of the constellation of LEO, together with those from the Sun, form the human heart. This heart is unique for each man and woman according to what each ego brings to that sphere.

The Spiritual Beings of the constellation of Aries form the future head.

The Hierarchies of Taurus, together with those of Mars, elaborate the region of the larynx. Each untruth that the man uttered in the last life has an effect on his future organs of speech from what is reflected upward from Mars forces.

These are just a hint of what the Spiritual Hierarchies of the constellations of the Zodiac do in building the spiritual seed of man's future physical body.

All of these forces are concentrated into a spiritual orb which is a miniature of the cosmic bodies of zodiacal constellations and the planetary system of our sun.

THE COSMIC MIDNIGHT

There comes a point in the spiritual worlds where the ego "is most steeped in spiritual light". Yet at this point, the ego experiences most that down there in the planetary sphere is the lasting record of all that he, man, did. He cannot abandon it. He, however, cannot alter it from that world. It can only be done by going

down to earth. This point is called
THE COSMIC MIDNIGHT, the
midpoint between death and the next
incarnation on earth.

    MAN, therefore, resolves to
return to the planetary spheres from
Saturn to Moon to earth. This is the
midpoint between death and rebirth.
For an adult, that rebirth will be
centuries later, in the regular course
of events. In many, many special
situations, the period is MUCH
shorter.

THE EGO'S RETURN FROM THE ZODIAC TOWARDS EARTH

From the vastness of the Zodiac, the ego condenses ever more and more. The sublime Spiritual Hierarchies implant into the spiritual seed of the physical body all the special   individual characteristics for each organ of the human body. These special organs are what all the previous lives of that ego require in order to counteract the deficiencies accumulated in those earthly lives, especially the last earth-life.

This is so because if the evil course is followed in two incarnations, it would enter into the etheric body and become ingrained as a habit.

An evil characteristic carried into the third incarnation results in a deformed physical organ. This may NOT be the cause in every case, so please do NOT go around making judgments.

THE SPIRITUAL ORB OF THE SEED OF THE PHYSICAL BODY

The spiritual seed takes the form of a miniature cosmos and it has living powers embedded in it. All the marvelous intricacies of each of our organs, such as the head which embodies in itself, all the secrets of the cosmos; the HEART which functions without stopping throughout life, be it twenty years, or a hundred and twenty years!

The larynx and lungs which can express sounds most soothing and loving; THE DIGESTIVE SYSTEM which can transform whatever food man takes in and demolish their original character and reassemble the parts into blood, muscle, bone, nerve, hormone, or whatever the body needs at any particular moment. The digestive system is in reality, a miracle system, if ever there is one.

So we can see that man's work in the cosmos, working with the spiritual hierarchies, is a task that exceeds any task that he can do on earth, no matter how great a scientist or inventor he becomes.

And to have all these hundreds of years of efforts of one's ego and that of the sublime Spiritual Hierarchies destroyed by a suicidal act, is a deed of utmost ignorance.

THE SPHERE OF THE OUTER PLANETS

When the sphere of Saturn is reached, the Archetypes of soul work creatively; in Jupiter, the Archetypes of life; in the Mars sphere, the Archetypes of the physical.

THE SUN SPHERE AND THE INNER PLANETS

After the sun sphere, the ego contracts to the size of the orbit of Mercury. The Archangels, who are the folk souls of the peoples and races, select the race into which the ego will incarnate in accordance with the ego's present needs.

In the next sphere, the Angelic guide of the ego assists in directing the ego to his parents. "The ego draws the person to the paternal part of the parents; the astral body draws him especially to the mother". The Yahweh Being leads man down to earth.

RETURN TO THE MOON SPHERE

It is important to the descending ego whether to incarnate in a male or female body. Due preparation must be made in the Moon sphere. In the previous earth-life, a dominant male incarnation would call for a female body in the following incarnation. However, there are special cases of significant egos where several succeeding incarnations in the same sex may take place before a balancing out in the other sex occurs.

A female incarnation would generally result in a male incarnation in the succeeding life.

When seen from the earth there is a full moon, the ego approaching earth at that time shall be attracted to a female body. When there is a new moon, seen from earth, the ego is attracted to a male body.

Those dominating males is this earth-life will not be too happy to learn that they will be females in their next incarnation. It surely would be a good reason to reject everything they read in this brief survey, BUT it won't do them any good: **They will still become females the next time they return to earth!** Of course, they in their higher consciousness in the spiritual world , will have, out of their own volition, decided to have it so.

THE NEW EARTH LIFE

While the ego is still above the earth, it sees its spirit orb of the physical body drop down to earth to unite with the germ seed in the mother's womb. In order to unite with it, the ego gathers the etheric body from the etheric forces in which it is surrounded. At about the third week, the ego/astral/etheric join the spirit orb in the developing embryo. In the seventh week, the etheric body becomes active; the astral body in the seventh month, and the ego before birth.

THE COSMIC SOURCE OF THE CHILD

According to our scientific view, father and mother are the sole creators of the child.

According to the Seer, father and mother are the LAST step in a long preparation that stretched out to the last life on earth, went through the re-experiencing of the last life intensely in the soul world, saw his errors there, developed powerful intentions to right the wrongs he had committed, progressed into the sublime worlds of spirit where Hierarchical Beings of specialized powers helped in building the spirit seed of the forthcoming physical body, and when no further progress could be made in the spirit world, the ego turned its gaze to the only place where it could make further progress in its development, and that is EARTH, where it could inhabit a physical body which is separated from all others.

In that separate body, it is possible to carry out its intentions,

THE REINCARNATING HUMAN BEING

Only through transforming the wisdom of the universe which flows to us abundantly, into life forces of the earthly structure do we approach the new incarnation in the right way. And when we come down to earth, we must have transformed so much wisdom into life forces, that we are able to permeate with enough spiritual life forces the hereditary substance that we receive from father and mother.

"The hereditary stream may not provide the ideal organism for the spirit. Certain adjustments are made by means of childhood diseases and the spiritual worlds work forcefully into the child, especially in the first three years before the child has consciousness of self. This is the point to which our memory can go back to in later life."

In those first years of life, the miracle of gaining the vertical position against the forces of gravity (with the help of the ARCHAI); acquiring the power of speech (with the help of the ARCHANGEL); and organizing the brain as an instrument for thinking (with the help of the ANGEL) take place. During the first three years, these spiritual beings are close to the child. The Seer can observe this as the aura which surrounds the child.

"After gaining self awareness and being able to say "I", the higher beings withdraw and the aura which extended around the child draws within him. This wisdom that works on the child in its first three years of earth life is never again as high after he becomes conscious of himself as an earth being", says Rudolf Steiner.

THE TEMPTERS OF MAN: LUCIFER and AHRIMAN

In order for man to develop into a completely FREE being, he must be able to choose between GOOD and EVIL. Therefore, GOD THE FATHER CREATOR permitted tempters to take part in mankind's development. There are two hordes of these tempters. One group, led by LUCIFER, brings man consciousness of himself in a selfish way. He wants to make man into a moral spiritual being quickly, and forsake earth development by going into a low spiritual existence, detached from higher spiritual beings. All future development planned by God would be negated, denied, stopped short in a blind alley.

LUCIFER'S AIMS

Lucifer gives man a prideful, egotistic feeling of himself. He cannot be seen by man, so he works insidiously. He is the one who takes hold of man's astral body, thereby debasing his passions, urges and desires. He makes man crave for impressions of the world.

AHRIMAN'S AIMS

Ahriman and his hordes, on the other hand, make man believe that everything in his environment is material. He hides from man the true spiritual foundation of stone, plant and animal. He is the FATHER OF LIES. He hides the fact that matter is a CONDENSATION OF SPIRIT.

Ahriman has worked on man since the middle of the Atlantean period. In our age, Ahriman has succeeded to a devastating extent, in that modern man in the highest institutions of learning to the lowliest person, ALL SEE NO SPIRIT behind everything that surrounds them in animal, plant and stone.

Scientists do not know that each species of animals has a group soul that exists in the astral world, and guides each species on earth.

These group souls are offspring of higher hierarchies. You can think of them as SUPERpuppeteers who guide the individual members of the species in their migrations over the face of the earth! Isn't that something for scientists to think about!

The details are too numerous to be taken further in this short description.

THE ETHERIC CHRIST

However, the materialistic view of creation and of the world, the solar system and the fixed stars of the universe is predominant. Even

Christ's words: "I am with you always, even until the end of earth days", indicating that He has become the Spirit of the Earth since the Mystery of Golgotha, when His blood flowed into the earth, is taken lightly by most Christians. They do not know what the Seer can see, and that is that Christ lives in the etheric sphere surrounding earth and that any man who is prepared in his soul, can see the Etheric Christ just as St. Paul saw Him while as Saul, he journeyed to persecute the Christians because they claimed that the Sun Being, Christ, had descended to earth and had lived three years in Jesus of Nazareth. Saul believed that the Sun Being remained in the sun. His vision of the Etheric Christ convinced him that the Sun Spirit had indeed descended to earth!

THE POWER OF AHRIMAN

On the return from the Zodiac to earth, the normal length of time is several hundred years. "Ahriman can shorten this period by as much as TWO HUNDRED YEARS". He does this in order to dull the consciousness of man as to his spiritual nature, and to make him more materialistic. Ahriman thus creates many human helpers on earth who will write as great scientists, philosophers, poets: in the sphere of the drama and the epic, in law, medicine, sociology. We already have innumerable numbers of these.

Of the scores of thousands of books published each year, can you find any that is not totally materialistic?

Everything in our culture: newspapers, magazines, radio and TV programs, our dominant sports culture point to an Ahrimanic emphasis on earth-life alone.

Our educational policy of separation of religion and state has resulted in a denial of religion. Under the pretense of freedom of religion, it results in a denial of God.

It ends in an education in immorality where students in every field strive only for the highest grade even by cheating. Just to get into the best colleges, cheating (the lying of Ahriman) is employed. This is then carried out into professional schools as law, medicine, banking, accounting and other fields of human activity, and eventually into life in all these professions.

So our country finds bankers galore stealing funds from their depositors, lawyers doing the same with their clients' funds, doctors and pharmacists raiding medicare funds for work not performed and supplies not delivered. Immorality is as rampant in this country as it is in the rest of the world.

The quick collapse of the atheistic old Soviet state should become a warning to the world that immorality cannot survive in a moral universe. Our world, our universe is a spiritual creation where moral laws are supreme and where altruistic love, beauty and goodness will prevail.

CURRENT IDEAS OF MODERN MAN

Modern man has varied ideas concerning death. Some religious people think that they go directly to "heaven" or to hell. Others think they may have to wait for judgment day before it is decided which direction they will be headed. Atheists and materialists probably think that when the body dies, nothing exists anymore. That is, death is the END. PERIOD!

Still others may think they come back as animals. They do NOT know that each man and woman has an EGO while living in this physical world.

In contrast, a single group-soul exists in the astral world for a whole species of animals.

Some people think that by killing believers of other religions gives them a reserved space in their paradise.

How diversely mankind has been separated by the retarded Luciferic hosts that exist in all the hierarchies!

WHAT IS NEEDED OF MANKIND

Spiritually awakened men and women are needed to add their forces to those of the good gods who serve the FATHER GOD by following GOD THE SON and the HOLY SPIRIT Who can teach mankind the truth of the spiritual origin of mankind.

Mankind now thinks that he evolved upwards from the apes. This is a very superficial view. It is based on the dimmed-down consciousness when man approached earth from the cosmos. The consciousness of the ego for hundreds of years while it lived as a spiritual being among the Hierarchical Beings of the constellations of the zodiac, was explained earlier as that of Intuition. Intuition is three stages HIGHER than our earthly thinking.

As the ego starts on his journey back to earth, it was shown that consciousness grows dimmer and dimmer, going to Inspiration where the spiritual beings are only a memory, to Imagination where they are only pictured.

On entering earthlife, consciousness has dimmed down to NO memory of the spiritual worlds and spiritual beings. INSTEAD,

AHRIMAN HAS NESTLED IN MAN'S INTELLECT!

Man on earth is cut off from his roots in the spirit. His task is to find his way back to his creator while he lives on earth. He has to take his start by means of his THINKING which is his most advanced faculty.

He has to feel a strong personal NEED, a hunger to know about his own spirit and its relationship to the spirit of the universe.

He must start searching and he will find the answer in all that ANTHROPOSOPHY (the science of the wisdom of man) has received from Dr. Rudolf Steiner.

MORE OF AHRIMAN'S PLANS

The Ahrimanic beings are extremely clever. They struggle to harden man, make him sclerotic. They continually wage war against the good Powers of Moon, Venus and Mercury for the possession of man. If a man is given up completely to his passions and leads a wild and dissolute life, then these Ahrimanic powers are able to tear these instincts from him at his death and keep them in his realm just below the surface of the earth in the elements of earth and water.

Their efforts over thousands of years have succeeded in producing a whole race of subhuman beings on earth. Ahrimans's aim is to snatch such a vast number of human beings to become subhuman beings, that the earth will not go forward into its evolving into more spiritual states for humanity's future evolution.

These subhuman Ahrimanic beings who live just below the surface of earth are the forces that work in tides, volcanic eruptions and earthquakes.

These volcanic forces which can blast off huge mountain tops, such as Mt. St. Helen's and Krakatoa and spread their shattered fragments and ash over vast areas and the devastating earthquakes which shake mountains and continents, meanwhile shattering man-made structures as if they were flimsy toys, make the most powerful man-made H-bomb and A-bomb look like children playthings.

LUCIFERIC BEINGS

The Luciferic beings whose bodies consist of air and warmth, are invisible to man who have not developed the requisite faculties to see into that world. However, their deeds in wind and weather in all their forms and ferocity and overwhelming power have caused havoc in all parts of the world. They also fight for man in order to make of him just "force, color and sound, but NO physical body. They battle continually with the good gods of Mars, Jupiter and Saturn."

MAN THE BATTLEGROUND

Man is a battleground of supersensible Beings, good and evil. Man is a prize who is being fought for in his earth life, as well as when he is asleep. Therefore, man in our age must learn of these facts from the Science of the Spirit, ANTHROPOSOPHY, from the works of its founder, DR. RUDOLF STEINER (1861-1925). English translations of his works number in the hundreds of volumes.

They must no longer be ignored. To do so would leave mankind unguarded from this powerful being who is destined to incarnate in human form in the near future.

AHRIMAN'S FORTHCOMING INCARNATION

Ahriman prepares extensively for his forthcoming incarnation on earth. He wants to be as successful as possible so as to trap as many human beings as he can. First of all, he wants mankind to believe that HE

DOES NOT EXIST. Right now, if you mention "Ahriman" to anyone, the answer will be "Ahriman who?" When you mention "Satan", the answer will probably be "Sagan?" That's hitting it pretty close.

Ahriman's plan to obliterate all knowledge that the cosmos is permeated with soul and spirit has succeeded to an unprecedented degree. He also works to divide humanity into as many nations, clans and groups as possible.

He will, in his incarnation, establish a huge occult school where anyone can have a low grade of supersensible experience. Whereas arduous training is required to gain supersensible faculties in a safe manner, those who shun long training, will flock to Ahriman's occult school and will quickly gain powers which they think is a great advance for them. Whereas all who train in the right way to develop sound supersensible organs to see into the spiritual world, see the SAME beings and events, those gaining vision by Ahriman's means will each see different events and beings. Therefore, strife will ensue.

A longer description is given in the author's book LIFE BEFORE BIRTH, LIFE ON EARTH, LIFE AFTER DEATH, so will not be repeated here.

REINCARNATION AND KARMA

The foregoing is an abbreviated summary of one life on earth to the next life on earth. It traces the path of the astral

body and ego from the moment of death when the etheric body gives the astral body and ego a panoramic picture of the last life backwards to birth. The etheric body embodying all that man thought, carries all these into the etheric cosmos. Men's thoughts on earth, thereby, form a part of the life forces of the cosmos. In the ego's journey through the constellations of the zodiac, his spiritual seed of his physical body is actually created by the divine hierarchies. So, he is in truth, created in the image of God whose "body" or realm encompasses the starry worlds.

The death to rebirth survey gave the reasons the ego returns to earth. That is REINCARNATION.

THE PURPOSE OF EARTHLIFE

EARTH is where man has a physical body. And it is ONLY in a physical body that he can develop freely into an independent being. That is, he is separate from everyone else. He can choose between good and evil. If he aligns himself with the evil beings, it is his own free choice and he must take the consequences. Even if the evil beings work to deceive him, it is his own duty to align himself with the good beings who are always ready to help him.

As a matter of fact, since the year 1899 when the dark age when the spiritual worlds were most closed to mankind, ended, mankind now lives in an age when the spirit worlds have become open. Seeking-mankind can now find revelations exceeding any revealed in the past because he, man, has developed to a potentially higher level.

THE CONSCIOUSNESS SOUL AGE

Mankind has entered the consciousness soul age since the last third of the nineteenth century. This the age when ETERNAL TRUTHS must become a part of each man and woman. Man must NOT sleep through this age and fail to remember, rediscover the spiritual worlds he passed through on his way back to this earth life. Ahriman must not be allowed to hoodwink him and thereby defeat the divine aim of creating the solar system for man to develop into THE SPIRITUAL HIERARCHY OF

MAN, the tenth hierarchy, one rank below the ANGELS, and eight ranks below the sublime Cherubim, The Spirits of Harmony, Who bring harmony between our planetary system and the surrounding systems, and nine ranks below the loftiest hierarchy, the Seraphim, the Spirits of Love.

REINCARNATION AS A LOGICAL PROCESS

Reincarnation of the EGO (man's eternal spirit) should be recognized as a logical fact arrived at by precise thinking. Earth and the solar system have taken millions and millions of years to develop to its present state. Are we to use it only once? If we build a house, would we live in it only one night?

If man lives on earth only one time, would he want to exist in that imperfect state forever? Does he think that at his stage of development, his descendants up to the nth generation would be proud of him as he is now? Or does he think that after death, he somehow keeps on becoming more and more perfect?

If man lived only once on earth and went to heaven or hell, how would twentieth century man live, or coexist with a man from Caesars' time? Or with a man who knows only stone age tools? Or does one think that all those human beings of former ages should be consigned to everlasting hell fire?

If God created all of them, did He intend to create ages and ages of human beings just to be permanent fire wood that burns and suffers eternally?

Come on, you modern educated, gold-tasseled, royally-robed and highly honored savants! Where is your humanity which assigns untold generations of developing humanity to eternal suffering?

Living only one life on earth and then spend the rest of eternity in hell? Would a wisdom-filled Deity plan such a dastardly inhuman condition or situation for His creation?

Undoubtedly "NO", must be the answer.

One chance, two chances to improve, three chances..........untold number of chances for each and every human being to improve and develop until he learns to become more and more alike, more akin to his Creator!

It is possible to give a survey of the creation of man starting from the spiritual to his present state, but it will take us too far afield from the subject of the tragedy of suicide.

However, I believe that enough reasons have been given to show the futility of suicide, and that there are unlimited opportunities for each and every human being to develop to the potential and example set by all the brave, courageous, loving members of our race who have reached lofty heights.

May I conclude this survey with

MY ORIGIN AND YOURS

Am I a speck of dust in cosmic space?
I THINK of God, Creator
    of the human race;
My EYES can scan
    the stars above;
My HEART can feel deep thoughts of
    love;
My EARS distinguish differences
    of tones
Of voices, orchestras, or babes
    or stones;
My HANDS caress, give aid,
    defend the weak;
My HOPES: all mankind
brotherhood will seek.
So puny as I am, I cannot

be a speck of sod:
My ORIGIN, my PROTOTYPE
is surely God!

And so is yours in north,
and yours in east,
And yours in south and west!
We all are members of a
unitary race,
All heirs of God's manifold
gifts and grace,

But who are battling the
world over, so far
Like selfish, vicious untamed brats at
constant war.
It's time to awake, time to awake,
Oh Man!
Awake to the tasks that God
dreamed for you
And predestined by your lofty
PROTOTYPE:
To develop into godlike beings

worthy of the divine PLAN,
To fulfill God's dreams of the
HEAVENLY HIERARCHY OF
MAN!

copyright ©
1992
PAUL E.CHU

World View Press
P.O. Box 1314
Englewood Cliffs, N.J. 07632

Please send

____ copies of **The Tragedy of Suicide** @ $10 ea. $_____

____ copies **Life Before Birth, Life on Earth, Life After Death** @ $5 ea. $_____
Postage & handling ($1.50 to ea. address) $_____
N.J. residents, please add sales tax $_____

Total enclosed $_____
NO C.O.D. please.
Name:_____
Street:_____
City, State, Zip:_____
_____

About the Author
Paul E. Chu
Born in Honolulu, Hawaii
B.A. '31 Columbia; M.A. '32 Columbia
Major: Chemical Engineering.
Minors: mathematics, chemistry, physics. Professional experience as research chemist, spectroscopist, statistician, inventor, businessman, author.

Developed and marketed Ultra Tone Magic Salve, a highly effective skin remedy widely used in Hawaii and the Pacific area during WWII.

Now has ready a method to MINIMIZE an Exxon Valdez type disaster;

a method to save more lives and property in fires;

a redesign of airplanes to save more lives in some plane crashes.

All these require huge corporations to build the required equipment.

****

After he had studied the works of Dr. Rudolf Steiner for about forty years, he published LIFE BEFORE BIRTH, LIFE ON EARTH, LIFE AFTER DEATH. He found early in his studies of those works, called ANTHROPOSOPHY, that they gave to a scientifically, mathematically trained mind which is unswayed by preconceived limitations of man's capabilities, ULTIMATE ANSWERS to the baffling questions relating to man's existence and destiny: how he was created, why he is here on earth, and where he is going. Now after 20 additional years, he has distilled from nearly 60 years of Anthroposophical studies, this resume of why it is THE TRAGEDY OF SUICIDE for all those who are discouraged and dismayed by the problems of life, to resort to this act.